The Old Farmer's Almanac 2010

ENGAGEMENT CALENDAR

Begin the new year square with every man.

–Robert B. Thomas, founder of
The Old Farmer's Almanac (1766–1846)

For appointments, notes, and reminders

Writer: Martie Majoros • *Calendar editor:* Heidi Stonehill • *Art director:* Margo Letourneau
Contributors: Janice Stillman, Mare-Anne Jarvela, Jack Burnett, Sarah Perreault, and Celeste Longacre

Astronomical events are given in U.S. Eastern Standard Time or U.S. Eastern Daylight Time.

Cover art: The Fields in July © Anda Styler, artist

About the cover artist:
Anda Styler lives in Sherman, Connecticut. Her award-winning paintings, which typically portray
New England landscapes, are exhibited in New England galleries and in collections across the country.
Combining shadow, light, and vibrant color to create mood, Anda strives to bring an excitement
to her work that reflects the world around her and nature's lasting beauty.

If you find this calendar, return it to:

Name _____

Address _____

Home/Work/Cell _____/_____/_____

The Old Farmer's Almanac, P.O. Box 520, Dublin, New Hampshire 03444
Publisher: Sherin Pierce

To order your copies of The Old Farmer's Almanac Engagement Calendar, call 800-ALMANAC
or visit our Web site at **Shop.Almanac.com.**

For wholesale information, contact Cindy Schlosser at 800-729-9265, ext. 126,
or Stacey Korpi, ext. 160.

PRINTED IN U.S.A.

ISBN-13: 978-1-57198-491-3

2010

JANUARY

S	M	T	W	T	F	S
					1	2
3	4	5	6	7	8	9
10	11	12	13	14	15	16
17	**18**	19	20	21	22	23
24	25	26	27	28	29	30
31						

FEBRUARY

S	M	T	W	T	F	S
	1	2	3	4	5	6
7	8	9	10	11	12	13
14	**15**	16	17	18	19	20
21	22	23	24	25	26	27
28						

MARCH

S	M	T	W	T	F	S
	1	2	3	4	5	6
7	8	9	10	11	12	13
14	15	16	17	18	19	20
21	22	23	24	25	26	27
28	29	30	31			

APRIL

S	M	T	W	T	F	S
				1	**2**	3
4	**5**	6	7	8	9	10
11	12	13	14	15	16	17
18	19	20	21	22	23	24
25	26	27	28	29	30	

MAY

S	M	T	W	T	F	S
						1
2	3	4	5	6	7	8
9	10	11	12	13	14	15
16	17	18	19	20	21	22
23	**24**	25	26	27	28	29
30	**31**					

JUNE

S	M	T	W	T	F	S
		1	2	3	4	5
6	7	8	9	10	11	12
13	14	15	16	17	18	19
20	21	22	23	24	25	26
27	28	29	30			

JULY

S	M	T	W	T	F	S
				1	2	3
4	5	6	7	8	9	10
11	12	13	14	15	16	17
18	19	20	21	22	23	24
25	26	27	28	29	30	31

AUGUST

S	M	T	W	T	F	S
1	2	3	4	5	6	7
8	9	10	11	12	13	14
15	16	17	18	19	20	21
22	23	24	25	26	27	28
29	30	31				

SEPTEMBER

S	M	T	W	T	F	S
			1	2	3	4
5	**6**	7	8	9	10	11
12	13	14	15	16	17	18
19	20	21	22	23	24	25
26	27	28	29	30		

OCTOBER

S	M	T	W	T	F	S
					1	2
3	4	5	6	7	8	9
10	**11**	12	13	14	15	16
17	18	19	20	21	22	23
24	25	26	27	28	29	30
31						

NOVEMBER

S	M	T	W	T	F	S
	1	2	3	4	5	6
7	8	9	10	**11**	12	13
14	15	16	17	18	19	20
21	22	23	24	**25**	26	27
28	29	30				

DECEMBER

S	M	T	W	T	F	S
			1	2	3	4
5	6	7	8	9	10	11
12	13	14	15	16	17	18
19	20	21	22	23	24	**25**
26	27	28	29	30	31	

125 Years Ago

JANUARY 1885

The hours, the days, the weeks, and the months are what the years are made of, and it is for us to fill them up the best we know how.

—The Old Farmer's Almanac

Mercury and You

When Mercury goes retrograde, its influence on our lives depends on the astrological sign that the planet is in at the time.

When Mercury is retrograde in Capricorn: Avoid buying, selling, or renting real estate. Expect problems with paperwork, packing, and movers. Reunite with family or take a vacation.

Current stage: Mercury is retrograde in Capricorn through January 15. It will be direct from January 15 through April 17.

A favorable January brings us a good year.

MONTHLY REMINDERS

_____
_____
_____
_____
_____
_____
_____
_____
_____

FULL MOON

JANUARY 30

Algonquin tribes called this month's full Moon the "Sun Has Not Strength to Thaw" Moon.

Houseplant Hints

❧

Here are some tips for healthy plants all year long:

■ To deter aphids, spray plants with a mixture of 1 quart water and ¼ teaspoon mild dish detergent.

■ If leaves turn brown, create a more humid environment. Mist the leaves daily with tepid water, and set the pot on a tray filled with pebbles. Add enough water to the tray to have it come up to just below the bottom of the pot.

■ When you clean the freshwater fish tank, save the water and use it for your houseplants.

■ Repot a houseplant if its leaves wilt between waterings and the roots are growing out of the pot's drainage hole.

December 2009 ❧ January 2010

28 *Monday*

The heart has its summer and its winter.

29 *Tuesday*

Drink peppermint tea to help relieve congestion from colds, calm an upset stomach, or aid digestion.

30 *Wednesday*

A group of turtles is called a dole.

31 *Thursday*

Full Long Nights Moon

I never think of the future. It comes soon enough.

–Albert Einstein, American physicist (1879–1955)

JANUARY • 2010

S	M	T	W	T	F	S
					1	2
3	4	5	6	7	8	9
10	11	12	13	14	15	16
17	18	19	20	21	22	23
24	25	26	27	28	29	30
31						

FEBRUARY • 2010

S	M	T	W	T	F	S
	1	2	3	4	5	6
7	8	9	10	11	12	13
14	15	16	17	18	19	20
21	22	23	24	25	26	27
28						

New Year's Day

Friday

1

*What's well begun,
is half done.*
–Horace (Quintus Horatius
Flaccus), Roman poet (65–8 B.C.)

For added flavor, use
beer instead of water
when making a stew.

Saturday

2

The cat loves fish
but hates water.

Sunday

3

REMINDERS

JANUARY

---

4 *Monday*

Egg-ucation:
It was once customary
for new brides in
France to break an egg
on the doorstep of
their new home for
good luck.

---

5 *Tuesday*

On this day in 1779,
explorer Zebulon
Montgomery Pike
was born.

---

6 *Wednesday*

Epiphany

*Strange to see how a
good dinner and
feasting reconciles
everybody.*
–Samuel Pepys, English writer
(1633–1703)

---

7 *Thursday*

Last Quarter

JANUARY • 2010

S	M	T	W	T	F	S
					1	2
3	4	5	6	7	8	9
10	11	12	13	14	15	16
17	18	19	20	21	22	23
24	25	26	27	28	29	30
31						

FEBRUARY • 2010

S	M	T	W	T	F	S
1	2	3	4	5	6	
7	8	9	10	11	12	13
14	15	16	17	18	19	20
21	22	23	24	25	26	27
28						

Friday **8**

*Do what you can
to show you care about
other people, and you
will make our world
a better place.*

*–Rosalynn Carter,
U.S. First Lady (b. 1927)*

Saturday **9**

There is never a Saturday
without some sunshine.

Sunday **10**

GREEN UP:
Idling your car
for more than 30
seconds to warm it up
wastes fuel and
increases emissions.

REMINDERS

JANUARY

11 *Monday*

*The critical period
in matrimony
is breakfast-time.*
*–Sir Alan Patrick Herbert,
English writer (1890–1971)*

12 *Tuesday*

Q. *What fish likes
to gossip?*
A. Largemouth bass

13 *Wednesday*

In Sweden, it is
traditional to take
down the Christmas
tree today
(St. Knut's day).

14 *Thursday*

A danger foreseen is
half escaped.

JANUARY • 2010

S M T W T F S
              1   2
3   4   5   6   7   8   9
10 11 12 13 14 15 16
17 18 19 20 21 22 23
24 25 26 27 28 29 30
31

FEBRUARY • 2010

S M T W T F S
1   2   3   4   5   6
7   8   9 10 11 12 13
14 15 16 17 18 19 20
21 22 23 24 25 26 27
28

New Moon

Friday **15**

Happy Birthday:

On their birthday,
Russian children
receive a special pie
with a message carved
into the crust.

Saturday **16**

**Benjamin Franklin's
Birthday**

Benjamin Franklin
has been honored
in 14 different halls
of fame.

Sunday **17**

REMINDERS

....
....
....
....
....
....

JANUARY

18 *Monday*

Martin Luther King Jr.'s Birthday (observed)

Man is man because he is free to operate within the framework of his destiny.

–Martin Luther King Jr., American civil rights leader (1929–68)

19 *Tuesday*

Adding cinnamon to your diet may help to control blood sugar levels.

20 *Wednesday*

To remove tomato stains from a plastic container, fill it with water and add one or two foaming denture-cleaning tablets.

21 *Thursday*

Cats with their tails up and fur raised indicate approaching wind—or a dog.

JANUARY • 2010

S	M	T	W	T	F	S
					1	2
3	4	5	6	7	8	9
10	11	12	13	14	15	16
17	18	19	20	21	22	23
24	25	26	27	28	29	30
31						

FEBRUARY • 2010

S	M	T	W	T	F	S
1	2	3	4	5	6	
7	8	9	10	11	12	13
14	15	16	17	18	19	20
21	22	23	24	25	26	27
28						

Friday **22**

On this day in 1984, the Macintosh computer was first advertised.

Saturday **23**

First Quarter

Sunday **24**

Under pressure, people admit to murder, setting fire to the village church, or robbing a bank, but never to being bores.

–Elsa Maxwell, American columnist (1883–1963)

REMINDERS

January

25 Monday

One large log burns two to three times longer than the same volume of smaller logs.

26 Tuesday

To remove a splinter from your skin, apply white glue. Allow the glue to dry and then peel it off—the splinter will come off with it.

27 Wednesday

Some cause happiness wherever they go; others, whenever they go.

–Oscar Wilde, Irish poet (1854–1900)

28 Thursday

To keep bacon from curling while frying, run it under cold water first.

JANUARY • 2010

S	M	T	W	T	F	S
					1	2
3	4	5	6	7	8	9
10	11	12	13	14	15	16
17	18	19	20	21	22	23
24	25	26	27	28	29	30
31						

FEBRUARY • 2010

S	M	T	W	T	F	S
	1	2	3	4	5	6
7	8	9	10	11	12	13
14	15	16	17	18	19	20
21	22	23	24	25	26	27
28						

Friday 29

*One should know
everything that
one says, but not say
everything that
one knows.*

–The Old Farmer's Almanac,
1901

Saturday 30

Full Wolf Moon

Sunday 31

If there is no snow before
January, there will be the
more in March and April.

REMINDERS

FEBRUARY with *The Old Farmer's Almanac*

125 Years Ago

FEBRUARY 1885

A change of food now and then seems to suit the taste of a cow as well as that of a man.

–The Old Farmer's Almanac

Mercury and You

When Mercury is retrograde in Aquarius:
Petty squabbles, misunderstandings, and misconnections abound. Know who your friends are; friendships are put at risk.

Current stage:
Mercury is direct through April 17. It is not retrograde in Aquarius this year.

If snowflakes increase in size, a thaw will follow.

MONTHLY REMINDERS

FULL MOON

FEBRUARY 28

Wishram tribes called this month's full Moon the "Shoulder to Shoulder Around the Fire" Moon.

Doggy Discipline

Even the most well-behaved of man's best friends may need some additional training now and then. Keep these tips in mind:

■ Reinforce good behavior immediately with lots of praise—and treats.

■ Discipline a dog right away—even within a few seconds after the "bad" behavior, the dog may not understand why it is being disciplined.

■ Before scolding a dog, go to it. Don't yell at the dog to come to you. The animal will associate a scolding with approaching you and will be reluctant to come when called the next time.

FEBRUARY

1 Monday

GREEN UP:
Hang light-color, loose-weave curtains to preserve privacy while still allowing daylight to enter the room.

2 Tuesday

Candlemas
Groundhog Day

Groundhog hairs are often used for making trout flies for fishing.

3 Wednesday

To ripen an avocado, place it in a bowl of flour.

4 Thursday

Craft is better than muscle.

FEBRUARY • 2010

S	M	T	W	T	F	S
	1	2	3	4	5	6
7	8	9	10	11	12	13
14	15	16	17	18	19	20
21	22	23	24	25	26	27
28						

MARCH • 2010

S	M	T	W	T	F	S
	1	2	3	4	5	6
7	8	9	10	11	12	13
14	15	16	17	18	19	20
21	22	23	24	25	26	27
28	29	30	31			

Last Quarter

Friday

5

Saturday

6

There is always one fine week in February.

Sunday

7

Egg-ucation:
To easily clean up a raw egg that has dropped on a tile or linoleum kitchen floor, sprinkle it with salt before wiping it up.

REMINDERS

FEBRUARY

8 *Monday*

Wind roaring in chimney, rain to come.

9 *Tuesday*

Regularly wipe your phone receiver with a disinfectant to prevent germs from spreading.

10 *Wednesday*

Happy Birthday:

In Nepal, parents rub a mixture of colored rice and yogurt onto the birthday child's forehead for good luck.

11 *Thursday*

On this day in 1899, Fort Logan, Montana, experienced a record low temperature of −61°F.

FEBRUARY • 2010   MARCH • 2010

S M T W T F S   S M T W T F S
      1 2 3 4 5 6   1 2 3 4 5 6
7 8 9 10 11 12 13   7 8 9 10 11 12 13
14 15 16 17 18 19 20   14 15 16 17 18 19 20
21 22 23 24 25 26 27   21 22 23 24 25 26 27
28   28 29 30 31

Abraham Lincoln's Birthday

Friday 12

Abe Lincoln was the first U.S. president who was not born in one of the original 13 colonies.

New Moon

Saturday 13

Valentine's Day

Sunday 14

Where there is great love, there are always miracles.

–Willa Cather, American writer (1873–1947)

REMINDERS

....

....

....

....

....

....

February

15 Monday

George Washington's
Birthday (observed)
National Flag of
Canada Day
Family Day (Alta., Ont.,
Sask., Can.)

16 Tuesday

Mardi Gras (Ala., La.)

The official state
flower of Louisiana is
the magnolia.

17 Wednesday

𝔄𝔰𝔥 𝔚𝔢𝔡𝔫𝔢𝔰𝔡𝔞𝔶

*A talent is formed in
stillness; a character, in
the world's torrent.*
–Johann Wolfgang von Goethe,
German poet (1749–1832)

18 Thursday

To make your own
brass polish, mix
equal parts of vinegar
and baking soda.

FEBRUARY • 2010   MARCH • 2010

S	M	T	W	T	F	S
	1	2	3	4	5	6
7	8	9	10	11	12	13
14	15	16	17	18	19	20
21	22	23	24	25	26	27
28						

S	M	T	W	T	F	S
	1	2	3	4	5	6
7	8	9	10	11	12	13
14	15	16	17	18	19	20
21	22	23	24	25	26	27
28	29	30	31			

Winter's back breaks about now.

Friday **19**

Charm: the quality in others that makes us more satisfied with ourselves.

–Henri-Frédéric Amiel, Swiss poet (1821–81)

Saturday **20**

Sunday of Orthodoxy
First Quarter

Sunday **21**

REMINDERS

....
....
....
....
....
....

February

22 *Monday*

On this day in 1630, Native Americans introduced English colonists to popcorn.

23 *Tuesday*

Clothes make the man.

24 *Wednesday*

For shinier hair, mix about one teaspoon of baking soda into the shampoo in your hand.

25 *Thursday*

Q. *What fish likes to catch a tan?*
A. Sunfish

FEBRUARY • 2010

S	M	T	W	T	F	S
	1	2	3	4	5	6
7	8	9	10	11	12	13
14	15	16	17	18	19	20
21	22	23	24	25	26	27
28						

MARCH • 2010

S	M	T	W	T	F	S
	1	2	3	4	5	6
7	8	9	10	11	12	13
14	15	16	17	18	19	20
21	22	23	24	25	26	27
28	29	30	31			

Heritage Day (Y.T., Can.)

Friday **26**

*Tact is, after all, a kind
of mind reading.*
–Sarah Orne Jewett, American
writer (1849–1909)

A change of fortune hurts a wise man no more than a change in the Moon.

Saturday **27**

Full Snow Moon

Sunday **28**

REMINDERS

....
....
....
....
....
....

125 Years Ago

MARCH 1885

A good toolhouse is a very handy place, and it offers a place to work on many a rainy day.

–The Old Farmer's Almanac

Mercury and You

When Mercury is retrograde in Pisces: Expect foggy thinking, daydreams, and escapism to be more prevalent. Practice creative pursuits, such as writing, dancing, or painting.

Current stage:
Mercury is direct through April 17. It is not retrograde in Pisces this year.

In March much snow,
To plants and trees much woe.

MONTHLY REMINDERS

To Hopi tribes, this month's full Moon was the "Whispering Wind" Moon.

Planting Time

If you're unsure when it is safe to begin planting your garden, try one of these techniques for testing the soil temperature and moisture:

- Dig up a handful of soil, squeeze it into a ball, and then drop it. If it crumbles and breaks into small pieces, the soil is ready. If it holds its shape or breaks into two clumps, the soil is too wet.

- Step on garden soil and then stand back. Look at your footprint. If it is shiny, the soil is still too wet. If it is dull, excess water has drained away and it is time to plant.

MARCH

1 *Monday*

The month that comes in good will go out bad.

2 *Tuesday*

Texas Independence Day
Town Meeting Day (Vt.)

The official state flower of Vermont is the red clover.

3 *Wednesday*

Add heat to your next meatloaf by mixing in a teaspoon of horseradish.

4 *Thursday*

Sing before breakfast, cry before night.

MARCH • 2010

S M T W T F S
          1 2 3 4 5 6
 7 8 9 10 11 12 13
14 15 16 17 18 19 20
21 22 23 24 25 26 27
28 29 30 31

APRIL • 2010

S M T W T F S
                1 2 3
 4 5 6 7 8 9 10
11 12 13 14 15 16 17
18 19 20 21 22 23 24
25 26 27 28 29 30

Friday

5

If stored dahlia tubers
are starting to dry out,
sprinkle them with
water.

Saturday

6

On this day in 1806,
poet Elizabeth Barrett
Browning was born.

Last Quarter

Sunday

7

REMINDERS

....

....

....

....

....

....

MARCH

8 *Monday*

**Commonwealth Day
(Canada)**

*Canada is a country
whose main exports
are hockey players and
cold fronts.*

–Pierre Trudeau, Canadian
prime minister (1919–2000)

9 *Tuesday*

**As the days grow longer,
the storms grow stronger.**

10 *Wednesday*

Egg-ucation:
A hen turns her egg
over about 50 times
a day to keep the
yolk from sticking
to the shell.

11 *Thursday*

GREEN UP:
Check all faucets
for leaks
and
repair
promptly,
if necessary.

MARCH • 2010

S M T W T F S
1 2 3 4 5 6
7 8 9 10 11 12 13
14 15 16 17 18 19 20
21 22 23 24 25 26 27
28 29 30 31

APRIL • 2010

S M T W T F S
1 2 3
4 5 6 7 8 9 10
11 12 13 14 15 16 17
18 19 20 21 22 23 24
25 26 27 28 29 30

Friday

12

When chopping dried fruit, rub the sides of the knife with butter to keep the fruit from sticking to the knife.

Saturday

13

The First Lady is an unpaid public servant elected by one person— her husband.

–Lady Bird Johnson,
U.S. First Lady (1912–2007)

Sunday

14

Daylight Saving Time begins at 2:00 A.M.

Remember to spring forward by setting your clocks ahead 1 hour.

REMINDERS

....
....
....
....
....

MARCH

15 *Monday*

Andrew Jackson Day
(Tenn.)
New Moon

16 *Tuesday*

*The more articulate one
is, the more dangerous
words become.*

—May Sarton, American writer
(1912–95)

17 *Wednesday*

St. Patrick's Day
Evacuation Day
(Suffolk Co., Mass.)

Before baking Irish
soda bread, it's
traditional to make a
cross on the loaf to
ward off evil spirits.

18 *Thursday*

If severe weather is
expected, place
plastic milk jugs over
pansies and other
early bloomers.

MARCH • 2010

S	M	T	W	T	F	S
	1	2	3	4	5	6
7	8	9	10	11	12	13
14	15	16	17	18	19	20
21	22	23	24	25	26	27
28	29	30	31			

APRIL • 2010

S	M	T	W	T	F	S
				1	2	3
4	5	6	7	8	9	10
11	12	13	14	15	16	17
18	19	20	21	22	23	24
25	26	27	28	29	30	

A peck of March dust is worth a king's ransom.

Friday 19

Vernal Equinox

The Sun crosses the equator on its northward path at 1:32 P.M. EDT today.

Saturday 20

On this day in 1685, composer Johann Sebastian Bach was born.

Sunday 21

REMINDERS

....
....
....
....
....
....
....

March

22 Monday

23 Tuesday

First Quarter

24 Wednesday

Dreams are
necessary to life.
–Anaïs Nin, French-born
American writer (1903–77)

25 Thursday

A March Sun sticks like
a lock of wool.

MARCH • 2010

S M T W T F S
1 2 3 4 5 6
7 8 9 10 11 12 13
14 15 16 17 18 19 20
21 22 23 24 25 26 27
28 29 30 31

APRIL • 2010

S M T W T F S
1 2 3
4 5 6 7 8 9 10
11 12 13 14 15 16 17
18 19 20 21 22 23 24
25 26 27 28 29 30

Friday **26**

Buy a few
houseplants—having
them around may
help to lower blood
pressure.

Saturday **27**

One hint is worth two bushels of advice.

–The Old Farmer's Almanac,
1894

Sunday **28**

Palm Sunday

To protect your house
from lightning, gather
hazel tree branches
today and put them in
a vase with water.

REMINDERS

....
....
....
....
....
....

29 *Monday*

Seward's Day (Alaska)
Full Worm Moon

30 *Tuesday*

First day of Passover

**Worries go down better
with soup than without.**

—Jewish proverb

31 *Wednesday*

During a waning Moon
(such as today's),
plant crops that grow
belowground.

1 *Thursday*

All Fools' Day

Q. *Why are people so
tired on April 1?*
A. Because they
have just finished a
31-day March.

APRIL • 2010							MAY • 2010						
S	M	T	W	T	F	S	S	M	T	W	T	F	S
				1	2	3							1
4	5	6	7	8	9	10	2	3	4	5	6	7	8
11	12	13	14	15	16	17	9	10	11	12	13	14	15
18	19	20	21	22	23	24	16	17	18	19	20	21	22
25	26	27	28	29	30		23	24	25	26	27	28	29
							30	31					

Good Friday
Pascua Florida Day

Friday

2

The official state
flower of Florida is the
orange blossom.

Snow in April
is manure.

Saturday

3

Easter

Sunday

4

Egg-ucation:
In general, brown eggs
come from hens with
red feathers and ear
lobes; white eggs,
from hens with white
feathers and ear lobes.

REMINDERS

....
....
....
....
....
....

125 Years Ago

APRIL 1885

Of course the land [has] to be fed. No use to try to get something out of nothing.

–The Old Farmer's Almanac

Mercury and You

When Mercury is retrograde in Aries:
Expect to be frustrated. Watch what you say and how you say it. Listen closely to what others have to say to you.

Current stage:
Mercury is direct through April 17.
It is not retrograde in Aries this year.
It is retrograde in Taurus from April 18 through May 11.

Till April's dead,
Change not a thread.

MONTHLY REMINDERS

The Northern Arapaho called this month's full Moon the "Ice Breaking in the River" Moon.

<u>AROUND THE HOUSE</u>

Earthy Easter Eggs

Experiment with some of these natural dyes if you want subtle, earth-tone Easter eggs. (Unless noted, soak the eggs in the mixture for at least 10 minutes.)

- Pink: 1 teaspoon vinegar mixed with 1 cup canned beet juice.

- Yellow: ¾ cup hot water, 1 teaspoon turmeric, and ½ teaspoon vinegar

- Orange-brown: Boil together ¾ cup water and 1 tablespoon chili powder. Let simmer for 30 minutes and add 1 teaspoon vinegar. Use dye while still hot.

- Brown: 1 cup cooled leftover coffee mixed with 1 teaspoon vinegar.

- Yellow-green: Save ¾ cup of the cooking water from 1 pound of asparagus. Add 1 tablespoon vinegar.

- Marbled tan: Layer onion skins around a raw egg to cover it completely. Wrap the egg in a single layer of cheesecloth and tie the loose ends together. Boil the egg as you would to make a hard-cooked egg.

APRIL

5 *Monday*

Easter Monday

Ideas should be clear,
and chocolate, thick.

–Spanish proverb

6 *Tuesday*

Last Quarter

7 *Wednesday*

GREEN UP:
Remove all
unnecessary items
from your car; extra
weight reduces gas
mileage.

8 *Thursday*

On this day in 1918,
U.S. First Lady Betty
Ford was born.

APRIL • 2010

S M T W T F S
          1 2 3
4 5 6 7 8 9 10
11 12 13 14 15 16 17
18 19 20 21 22 23 24
25 26 27 28 29 30

MAY • 2010

S M T W T F S
                1
2 3 4 5 6 7 8
9 10 11 12 13 14 15
16 17 18 19 20 21 22
23 24 25 26 27 28 29
30 31

To make a cake with a
light consistency,
cream the butter and
sugar thoroughly.

Friday

9

An earthworm can
aerate about one-half
pound of soil per day.

Saturday

10

*Of course we
weren't lost. We were
merely where we
shouldn't have been
without knowing where
that was.*

—T. Morris Longstreth,
American writer (1886–1975)

Sunday

11

REMINDERS

....

....

....

....

....

....

April

12 *Monday*

Don't count your fish until they're on dry land.

13 *Tuesday*

Thomas Jefferson's Birthday

During his lifetime, Jefferson wrote nearly 20,000 letters.

14 *Wednesday*

New Moon

15 *Thursday*

A society grows great when old men plant trees whose shade they know they shall never sit in.

—Greek proverb

APRIL • 2010	MAY • 2010
S M T W T F S	S M T W T F S
1 2 3	1
4 5 6 7 8 9 10	2 3 4 5 6 7 8
11 12 13 14 15 16 17	9 10 11 12 13 14 15
18 19 20 21 22 23 24	16 17 18 19 20 21 22
25 26 27 28 29 30	23 24 25 26 27 28 29
	30 31

Friday **16**

To help control
aphids, plant anise
and coriander in
your garden.

Saturday **17**

*The only athletic sport
I ever mastered was
backgammon.*
–Douglas William Jerrold,
English writer (1803–57)

Sunday **18**

Happy Birthday:
In Sweden, children
receive breakfast in
bed on their birthday.

REMINDERS

....
....
....
....
....
....

APRIL

19 Monday

Patriots Day (Maine, Mass.)

The official state
flower of Maine is
the white pine cone
and tassel.

20 Tuesday

If pigeons return
home slowly, the weather
will be wet.

21 Wednesday

San Jacinto Day (Tex.)
First Quarter

22 Thursday

Earth Day

*Mountains are
Earth's undecaying
monuments.*

–Nathaniel Hawthorne,
American writer (1804–64)

APRIL • 2010

S	M	T	W	T	F	S
				1	2	3
4	5	6	7	8	9	10
11	12	13	14	15	16	17
18	19	20	21	22	23	24
25	26	27	28	29	30	

MAY • 2010

S	M	T	W	T	F	S
						1
2	3	4	5	6	7	8
9	10	11	12	13	14	15
16	17	18	19	20	21	22
23	24	25	26	27	28	29
30	31					

St. George's Day (N.L., Can.)

Friday **23**

To attract bees, plant chives in the garden.

Birthday of Robert B. Thomas (1766–1846), founder of *The Old Farmer's Almanac*

Saturday **24**

Q. *Why did the hens stop laying eggs?*
A. They got tired of working for chicken feed.

Sunday **25**

REMINDERS

26 *Monday*

To ripen bananas,
wrap them in a damp
paper towel and keep
them in a paper bag.

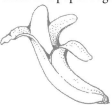

27 *Tuesday*

On this day in 1947,
Babe Ruth Day was
first celebrated at
Yankee Stadium.

28 *Wednesday*

Full Pink Moon

29 *Thursday*

*Cut a few straws from a
new broom to use
later for testing cakes.*
—The Old Farmer's Almanac,
1926

	APRIL • 2010								MAY • 2010				
S M T W T F S							S M T W T F S						
				1	2	3							1
4	5	6	7	8	9	10	2	3	4	5	6	7	8
11	12	13	14	15	16	17	9	10	11	12	13	14	15
18	19	20	21	22	23	24	16	17	18	19	20	21	22
25	26	27	28	29	30		23	24	25	26	27	28	29
							30	31					

National Arbor Day

Friday **30**

*Let us give nature
a chance; she knows
her business better
than we do.*

–Michel Eyquem de Montaigne,
French writer (1533–92)

May Day

Saturday **1**

**Hoar frost today indicates
a good harvest.**

Egg-ucation:
May is National
Egg Month.

Sunday **2**

REMINDERS

....
....
....
....
....
....

125 Years Ago

MAY 1885

Spring comes but once a year; and the only way is to fly 'round and make the most of it.

–The Old Farmer's Almanac

Mercury and You

When Mercury is retrograde in Taurus: Take time to formulate your thoughts. Delay money matters; review financial affairs and position yourself for growth.

Current stage: Mercury is retrograde in Taurus through May 11. It will be direct from May 12 through August 19.

When sheep turn their backs to the wind, it is a sign of rain.

MONTHLY REMINDERS

Cherokee tribes called this month's full Moon the "Planting" Moon.

AROUND THE HOUSE

Butterfly Garden

To attract butterflies to your garden, plant these nectar-rich flowers:

- Aster
- Bee balm
- Black-eyed Susan
- Cosmos
- Foxglove
- Globe thistle
- Hosta
- Joe-Pye weed
- Lavender
- Lilac
- Milkweed
- Phlox
- Sedum
- Thyme
- Verbena
- Yarrow

MAY

3 Monday

It is one of my sources of happiness never to desire a knowledge of other people's business.

—Dolley Madison, U.S. First Lady (1768–1849)

4 Tuesday

To ease a sinus infection, sip some oregano tea.

5 Wednesday

Cinco de Mayo

The green tree frog becomes very unquiet before rain.

6 Thursday

Last Quarter

| MAY • 2010 | | | | | | | | JUNE • 2010 | | | | | |
S	M	T	W	T	F	S		S	M	T	W	T	F	S
						1				1	2	3	4	5
2	3	4	5	6	7	8		6	7	8	9	10	11	12
9	10	11	12	13	14	15		13	14	15	16	17	18	19
16	17	18	19	20	21	22		20	21	22	23	24	25	26
23	24	25	26	27	28	29		27	28	29	30			
30	31													

Friday 7

Plan a garden border
that is at least 5 feet
wide; narrower beds
dry out more quickly.

Saturday 8

Truman Day (Mo.)

The official state
flower of Missouri is
the hawthorn.

Sunday 9

Mother's Day

**A mother understands
what a child does not say.**

—Jewish proverb

REMINDERS

....
....
....
....
....
....

May

10 *Monday*

GREEN UP:
Unplug electronic devices when not in use. Some, such as DVD players, use electricity even when turned off.

11 *Tuesday*

Common mud is still the best remedy for bee or wasp stings.

12 *Wednesday*

On this day in 1982, Coal Creek Canyon in the Colorado Rockies received 46 inches of snow.

13 *Thursday*

New Moon

MAY • 2010   JUNE • 2010

S M T W T F S   S M T W T F S
          1   1 2 3 4 5
2 3 4 5 6 7 8   6 7 8 9 10 11 12
9 10 11 12 13 14 15   13 14 15 16 17 18 19
16 17 18 19 20 21 22   20 21 22 23 24 25 26
23 24 25 26 27 28 29   27 28 29 30
30 31

Friday 14

A curdly sky will not be
24 hours dry.

Saturday 15

Armed Forces Day

*'Tis the soldiers' life
to have their balmy
slumbers waked
with strife.*

–William Shakespeare,
English writer (1564–1616)

Sunday 16

Q. *What fish goes well
with peanut butter?*
A. Jellyfish

REMINDERS

May

17 Monday

I'm living so far beyond my income that we may almost be said to be living apart.

—e. e. cummings, American poet
(1894–1962)

18 Tuesday

The official state cultivated flower of Tennessee is the iris.

19 Wednesday

When a cow tries to scratch its ear,
It means a shower is very near.

20 Thursday

First Quarter

MAY • 2010

S	M	T	W	T	F	S
						1
2	3	4	5	6	7	8
9	10	11	12	13	14	15
16	17	18	19	20	21	22
23	24	25	26	27	28	29
30	31					

JUNE • 2010

S	M	T	W	T	F	S
		1	2	3	4	5
6	7	8	9	10	11	12
13	14	15	16	17	18	19
20	21	22	23	24	25	26
27	28	29	30			

Friday 21

Cut plastic bags into strips and use them to tie plants to poles or trellises in the garden.

National Maritime Day

Saturday 22

Ocean: A body of water occupying about two-thirds of a world made for man—who has no gills.

–Ambrose Bierce, American writer (1842–c. 1914)

Whitsunday–Pentecost

Sunday 23

For sunburn relief, apply mayonnaise to the affected area.

REMINDERS

....
....
....
....
....
....

May

24 *Monday*

Victoria Day (Canada)

Canada is a country that works better in practice than in theory.

–Stéphane Dion, Quebec politician (b. 1955)

25 *Tuesday*

To polish brass, rub it with wood ashes moistened with oil.

26 *Wednesday*

Seaweed is an excellent fertilizer for citrus fruit and roses.

27 *Thursday*

Full Flower Moon

MAY • 2010								JUNE • 2010					
S	M	T	W	T	F	S		S	M	T	W	T	F	S
						1				1	2	3	4	5
2	3	4	5	6	7	8		6	7	8	9	10	11	12
9	10	11	12	13	14	15		13	14	15	16	17	18	19
16	17	18	19	20	21	22		20	21	22	23	24	25	26
23	24	25	26	27	28	29		27	28	29	30			
30	31													

Friday **28**

On this day in 1957, baseball player Kirk Gibson was born.

Saturday **29**

We should consider every day lost on which we have not danced at least once.

–Friedrich Nietzsche, German philosopher (1844–1900)

Sunday **30**

A dream of docile bees foretells good fortune to come.

REMINDERS

MAY ✤ JUNE

31 *Monday*

Memorial Day (observed)

There are about 250
species of poppies.

1 *Tuesday*

*There isn't much that
tastes better than praise
from those who are wise
and capable.*

—Selma Lagerlöf, Swedish writer
(1858–1940)

2 *Wednesday*

**If June be sunny,
harvest comes early.**

3 *Thursday*

A mixture of lemon
juice and salt will help
to remove rust stains
from fabric.

JUNE • 2010

S	M	T	W	T	F	S
		1	2	3	4	5
6	7	8	9	10	11	12
13	14	15	16	17	18	19
20	21	22	23	24	25	26
27	28	29	30			

JULY • 2010

S	M	T	W	T	F	S
				1	2	3
4	5	6	7	8	9	10
11	12	13	14	15	16	17
18	19	20	21	22	23	24
25	26	27	28	29	30	31

Last Quarter

Friday

4

World Environment Day

Saturday

5

GREEN UP:
Deciduous trees on the south side of your house will provide shade in summer and allow the Sun to warm your house in winter.

Sunday

6

Cats are able to produce about 100 different vocalized sounds. Dogs? Only about 10.

REMINDERS

125 Years Ago

JUNE 1885

Sow corn for fodder in rows from 3 to 4 feet apart, at the rate of 3 pecks of seed to the acre.

–The Old Farmer's Almanac

Mercury and You

When Mercury is retrograde in Gemini:
Be prepared for miscommunications; expect lots of phone calls, or none, and lost or misplaced mail. Gossip abounds.

Current stage:
Mercury is direct through August 19. It is not retrograde in Gemini this year.

If the flowers keep open all night, the weather will be wet the next day.

MONTHLY REMINDERS

FULL MOON

JUNE 26

To Cree tribes, this month's full Moon was known as the "Month Leaves Come Out" Moon.

Painting Pointers

❧

These simple tips will make painting your house a lot easier.

■ To keep bugs away when painting outdoors, add a few drops of citronella to the paint.

■ Avoid overloading your brush with paint. Dip only half the length of the bristles into the paint and then gently tap the brush on the side of the can to remove any excess.

■ To make it easier to remove hardened paint on windowpanes, spray hot vinegar on the paint.

■ If the outside of your house needs more than one coat of paint, put on one this year and then wait until next year to give it a second coat. The paint will be less likely to peel.

■ When painting stairs, start by painting every other step. When these are dry, paint the remaining ones. You will still be able to use the stairs.

JUNE

7 Monday

Don't open a shop unless you know how to smile.

—Jewish proverb

8 Tuesday

On this day in 1940, the bald eagle was identified as an endangered species in the United States.

9 Wednesday

Q. *How do billboards communicate?*
A. Sign language

10 Thursday

When black snails on the road you see,
Then on the morrow rain will be.

JUNE • 2010

S	M	T	W	T	F	S
		1	2	3	4	5
6	7	8	9	10	11	12
13	14	15	16	17	18	19
20	21	22	23	24	25	26
27	28	29	30			

JULY • 2010

S	M	T	W	T	F	S
				1	2	3
4	5	6	7	8	9	10
11	12	13	14	15	16	17
18	19	20	21	22	23	24
25	26	27	28	29	30	31

King Kamehameha I Day (Hawaii)

Friday **11**

The official state
flower of Hawaii is the
yellow pua aloalo
(hibiscus).

New Moon

Saturday **12**

There are about
450 feet of wool yarn
in a baseball.

Sunday **13**

REMINDERS

JUNE

14 *Monday*

Flag Day

On this day in 1877,
Flag Day was
observed nationally
for the first time.

15 *Tuesday*

The sudden storm
lasts not 3 hours.

16 *Wednesday*

Egg-ucation:
For fluffier egg whites,
let them warm to
room temperature
before beating.

17 *Thursday*

Bunker Hill Day
(Suffolk Co., Mass.)

The current Bunker
Hill monument was
dedicated on this day
in 1843.

JUNE • 2010	JULY • 2010
S M T W T F S	S M T W T F S
1 2 3 4 5	1 2 3
6 7 8 9 10 11 12	4 5 6 7 8 9 10
13 14 15 16 17 18 19	11 12 13 14 15 16 17
20 21 22 23 24 25 26	18 19 20 21 22 23 24
27 28 29 30	25 26 27 28 29 30 31

Friday **18**

The bluebonnet is the state flower of Texas.

Saturday **19**

Emancipation Day (Tex.)
First Quarter

Sunday **20**

Father's Day
West Virginia Day

*It doesn't matter
who my father was;
it matters who I
remember he was.*

–Anne Sexton, American poet
(1928–74)

REMINDERS

....
....
....
....
....

June

21 Monday

National Aboriginal Day
(Canada)
Summer Solstice

*The summer night
is like a perfection
of thought.*
−Wallace Stevens, American poet
(1879–1955)

22 Tuesday

On this day in 1868,
Arkansas was
readmitted to the
Union.

23 Wednesday

To remove chewing
gum from hair, apply
peanut butter to the
area, rub into the gum,
and wash hair as usual.

24 Thursday

Discovery Day (N.L., Can.)
Fête Nationale (Qué., Can.)

Quebec City received
its name from the
Algonquin word
kebek, referring to a
strait or channel that
narrows.

JUNE • 2010   JULY • 2010

S M T W T F S   S M T W T F S
        1 2 3 4 5   1 2 3
6 7 8 9 10 11 12   4 5 6 7 8 9 10
13 14 15 16 17 18 19   11 12 13 14 15 16 17
20 21 22 23 24 25 26   18 19 20 21 22 23 24
27 28 29 30   25 26 27 28 29 30 31

*When you get to the
end of your rope, tie a
knot and hang on.*

*–Franklin Delano Roosevelt,
32nd U.S. president (1882–1945)*

Friday **25**

Full Strawberry Moon

Saturday **26**

Happy Birthday:

On their birthday,
children in Brazil
receive a tug on
the ear for each year
of age.

Sunday **27**

REMINDERS

....

....

....

....

....

JUNE ❧ JULY

28 Monday

Love is like mushrooms. One doesn't know if they belong to the good or bad sort until it is too late.

—Tristan Bernard, French writer (1866–1947)

29 Tuesday

Time spent laughing is time spent with the gods.

—Japanese proverb

30 Wednesday

To open up a slow drain, drop two seltzer tablets and a cup of vinegar down it. After about 5 minutes, rinse with hot water.

1 Thursday

Canada Day

Economics is extremely useful as a form of employment for economists.

—John Kenneth Galbraith, Canadian-born U.S. economist (1908–2006)

JULY • 2010   AUGUST • 2010

S	M	T	W	T	F	S
				1	2	3
4	5	6	7	8	9	10
11	12	13	14	15	16	17
18	19	20	21	22	23	24
25	26	27	28	29	30	31

S	M	T	W	T	F	S
1	2	3	4	5	6	7
8	9	10	11	12	13	14
15	16	17	18	19	20	21
22	23	24	25	26	27	28
29	30	31				

In 1979, the Georgia State Capitol dome was covered with 60 ounces of gold.

Friday

2

Q. *What did the beach say when the tide came in?*
A. Long time, no sea.

Saturday

3

Independence Day
Last Quarter

Sunday

4

REMINDERS

....
....
....
....
....

125 Years Ago

JULY 1885

In the busy days of this hot month, we must not forget that the henhouse needs some care.

–The Old Farmer's Almanac

Mercury and You

When Mercury is retrograde in Cancer:
Expect annoyances with baking,
other household duties, and gardening.
Complete unfinished projects.

Current stage:
Mercury is direct until August 19.
It is not retrograde in Cancer this year.

Generally, a moist and cool summer portends a hard winter.

MONTHLY REMINDERS

Omaha tribes called this month's full Moon the "Moon When the Buffalo Bellow."

Pack-a-Picnic

In addition to the food, drinks, utensils, napkins, and plates for your picnic, don't forget to bring these items:

- Adhesive bandages
- Binoculars
- Blanket, quilt, or folding chairs
- Camera
- Citronella candles
- Flashlight, for evening picnics
- Hat
- Insect repellent
- Kites, Frisbees, or balls
- Paper towels
- Sunglasses
- Sunscreen
- Tablecloth
- Trash bags

JULY

5   *Monday*

What do we live for,
if it is not to make
life less difficult for
each other?

—George Eliot, English writer
(1819–80)

6   *Tuesday*

In hotels, the
third through sixth
floors are the safest
from burglars and
can be reached easily
with a fire ladder,
if needed.

7   *Wednesday*

Store dairy products
in the coldest part
of the refrigerator—in
the back, away from
the door.

8   *Thursday*

**If bats fly abroad after
sunset, expect fair weather.**

JULY • 2010   AUGUST • 2010

S	M	T	W	T	F	S
				1	2	3
4	5	6	7	8	9	10
11	12	13	14	15	16	17
18	19	20	21	22	23	24
25	26	27	28	29	30	31

S	M	T	W	T	F	S
1	2	3	4	5	6	7
8	9	10	11	12	13	14
15	16	17	18	19	20	21
22	23	24	25	26	27	28
29	30	31				

Nunavut Day (Canada)

Friday 9

Nunavut means "our land" in the Inuktitut language.

People who keep journals have life twice.

–Jessamyn West, American writer (1902–84)

Saturday 10

New Moon

Sunday 11

REMINDERS

....

....

....

....

....

....

July

12 Monday

**Orangemen's Day
(N.L., Can.)**

The official
provincial flower of
Newfoundland is the
pitcher plant.

13 Tuesday

Cover raspberry
bushes with netting to
prevent birds from
eating the berries.

14 Wednesday

To remove ink stains
from washable cloth,
soak the fabric in
sour milk overnight;
in the morning, wash
with soap.

15 Thursday

One toad can eat
as many as 10,000
insects in one summer.

JULY • 2010

S	M	T	W	T	F	S
				1	2	3
4	5	6	7	8	9	10
11	12	13	14	15	16	17
18	19	20	21	22	23	24
25	26	27	28	29	30	31

AUGUST • 2010

S	M	T	W	T	F	S
1	2	3	4	5	6	7
8	9	10	11	12	13	14
15	16	17	18	19	20	21
22	23	24	25	26	27	28
29	30	31				

On this day in 1911, dancer Ginger Rogers was born.

Friday 16

Egg-ucation:
An egg will age more in one day at room temperature than it will in one week in the refrigerator.

Saturday 17

First Quarter

Sunday 18

REMINDERS

July

19 Monday

Be not stingy of kind words and pleasant acts.
–The Old Farmer's Almanac, 1894

20 Tuesday

GREEN UP:
To minimize watering, landscape with plants that are native to your region.

21 Wednesday

Nothing dries sooner than a tear.
–*Cicero, Roman statesman (106–43 B.C.)*

22 Thursday

Q. *What fish is the most valuable?*
A. Goldfish

JULY • 2010

S	M	T	W	T	F	S
				1	2	3
4	5	6	7	8	9	10
11	12	13	14	15	16	17
18	19	20	21	22	23	24
25	26	27	28	29	30	31

AUGUST • 2010

S	M	T	W	T	F	S
1	2	3	4	5	6	7
8	9	10	11	12	13	14
15	16	17	18	19	20	21
22	23	24	25	26	27	28
29	30	31				

Friday 23

To "fix" a crack in a vase, pour melted paraffin over the leaky spot and let it harden.

Saturday 24

Pioneer Day (Utah)

The official state flower of Utah is the sego lily.

Sunday 25

Full Buck Moon

REMINDERS

....
....
....
....
....
....

26 Monday

Cut hay just after
the full Moon.

27 Tuesday

*The profession of book
writing makes horse
racing seem like a solid
and stable business.*
–John Steinbeck, American writer
(1902–68)

28 Wednesday

To ease a headache,
lean your head against a
tree and have someone else
drive a nail into the
opposite side of the tree.

29 Thursday

*Rise and shine,
swimming's fine.*
–The Old Farmer's Almanac,
1952

JULY • 2010

S M T W T F S
          1 2 3
4 5 6 7 8 9 10
11 12 13 14 15 16 17
18 19 20 21 22 23 24
25 26 27 28 29 30 31

AUGUST • 2010

S M T W T F S
1 2 3 4 5 6 7
8 9 10 11 12 13 14
15 16 17 18 19 20 21
22 23 24 25 26 27 28
29 30 31

To help prevent
motion sickness, take
powdered ginger
capsules as directed.

Friday **30**

*I am always at a loss
to know how much
to believe of my own
stories.*

*–Washington Irving, American
writer (1783–1859)*

Saturday **31**

Routinely pinch back
basil plants to keep
them bushy.

Sunday **1**

REMINDERS

....

....

....

....

....

AUGUST with *The Old Farmer's Almanac*

125 *Years Ago*

AUGUST 1885

Give the boys a few days off and let them take a run to the seashore . . . to get a sniff of the salt sea breeze.

–The Old Farmer's Almanac

Mercury and You

When Mercury is retrograde in Leo:
Analyze your investment portfolio but avoid speculative investments. It is not a good time to buy, sell, or trade.

Current stage:
Mercury is direct through August 19.
It is not retrograde in Leo this year.
It is retrograde in Virgo from August 20 through September 12.

Plenty of berries indicates a severe winter.

MONTHLY REMINDERS

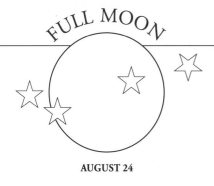

FULL MOON

AUGUST 24

The Cree called this month's full Moon the "Moon When Young Ducks Begin to Fly."

AROUND THE HOUSE

Sweet Dreams

❦

If getting a good night's sleep seems impossible, here are a few tips for a full night's rest:

■ Try to yawn—then yawn again. Yawning makes you feel sleepy.

■ Use all-cotton sheets. Some polyester-cotton blends are treated with formaldehyde, which can keep you awake.

■ Play a recording of something that you find soothing, such as the sound of waves breaking on the shore.

■ Make a 2x6-inch eye pillow out of silk or cotton fabric and fill it with dried lavender. Drape it over your eyes to encourage sleep.

■ Recite something that you know by heart—the Pledge of Allegiance, a prayer, a poem—and focus on taking deep, slow breaths.

AUGUST

2 *Monday*

Colorado Day
Civic Holiday (Canada)

*Go west, young man,
and grow up with
the country.*

–John B. L. Soule, American
newspaper editor (1815–91)

3 *Tuesday*

Last Quarter

4 *Wednesday*

A watermelon is about
92 percent water.

5 *Thursday*

Expect to receive some
money if you find a spider
in your pocket.

AUGUST • 2010

S	M	T	W	T	F	S
1	2	3	4	5	6	7
8	9	10	11	12	13	14
15	16	17	18	19	20	21
22	23	24	25	26	27	28
29	30	31				

SEPTEMBER • 2010

S	M	T	W	T	F	S
			1	2	3	4
5	6	7	8	9	10	11
12	13	14	15	16	17	18
19	20	21	22	23	24	25
26	27	28	29	30		

Friday

6

GREEN UP:
If possible, do errands during nonpeak hours to avoid idling your car's engine in heavy traffic.

Saturday

7

Paintin' is not important. The important thing is keepin' busy.

–Anna Mary Robertson "Grandma" Moses, American painter (1860–1961)

Sunday

8

Egg-ucation:
The largest chicken egg ever laid weighed 1 pound.

REMINDERS

AUGUST

9   *Monday*

New Moon

10   *Tuesday*

On this day in 1874, President Herbert Hoover was born.

11   *Wednesday*

First day of Ramadan

After an unusual fall of meteors, expect dry weather.

12   *Thursday*

Q. *What fish can perform operations?*
A. Sturgeon

AUGUST • 2010

S	M	T	W	T	F	S
1	2	3	4	5	6	7
8	9	10	11	12	13	14
15	16	17	18	19	20	21
22	23	24	25	26	27	28
29	30	31				

SEPTEMBER • 2010

S	M	T	W	T	F	S
			1	2	3	4
5	6	7	8	9	10	11
12	13	14	15	16	17	18
19	20	21	22	23	24	25
26	27	28	29	30		

Today is International Left-Handers Day.

Friday 13

Do not put off till tomorrow what can be put off till day-after-tomorrow just as well.

–Mark Twain, American writer (1835–1910)

Saturday 14

For juicier steaks, wait until they are nearly cooked before seasoning them with salt.

Sunday 15

REMINDERS

August

16 *Monday*

Bennington Battle Day (Vt.)
Discovery Day (Y.T., Can.)
First Quarter

17 *Tuesday*

In the dark,
all cats are gray.

18 *Wednesday*

When substituting
cultivated blueberries
for wild blueberries
in a recipe,
slightly increase the
amount of sugar.
Wild blueberries are
sweeter.

19 *Thursday*

National Aviation Day

"Hot" stars appear
blue; "warm" ones,
white; and "cool"
ones, yellow, orange,
or red.

AUGUST • 2010   SEPTEMBER • 2010

S M T W T F S   S M T W T F S
1 2 3 4 5 6 7   1 2 3 4
8 9 10 11 12 13 14   5 6 7 8 9 10 11
15 16 17 18 19 20 21   12 13 14 15 16 17 18
22 23 24 25 26 27 28   19 20 21 22 23 24 25
29 30 31   26 27 28 29 30

Friday **20**

For good luck,
always enter a new house
with a loaf of bread and
a new broom.

Saturday **21**

Happy Birthday:

In Guyana, it is
traditional to serve a
curry made from
chicken, duck, or
lamb at birthday
celebrations.

Sunday **22**

*A rose is sweeter in the
bud than full-blown.*
   *–John Lyly, English writer
      (c. 1554–1606)*

REMINDERS

....
....
....
....
....
....

AUGUST

23 *Monday*

To rid a room of smoke odor, soak a towel in equal parts vinegar and water, wring it out, and swish it around the room.

24 *Tuesday*

Full Sturgeon Moon

25 *Wednesday*

Health is the daughter of Exercise and Temperance.

26 *Thursday*

Women's Equality Day

. . . remember the Ladies, and be more generous and favorable to them than your ancestors.

–*Abigail Adams, U.S. First Lady (1744–1818), to John Adams about lawmaking*

AUGUST • 2010   SEPTEMBER • 2010

S	M	T	W	T	F	S
1	2	3	4	5	6	7
8	9	10	11	12	13	14
15	16	17	18	19	20	21
22	23	24	25	26	27	28
29	30	31				

S	M	T	W	T	F	S
			1	2	3	4
5	6	7	8	9	10	11
12	13	14	15	16	17	18
19	20	21	22	23	24	25
26	27	28	29	30		

Friday 27

Just in case:
When you travel out
of the country, bring
an extra pair of
eyeglasses.

Saturday 28

An ear of corn
contains from 600 to
800 kernels.

Sunday 29

If sunset on Sunday
is cloudy,
it will rain before
Wednesday.

REMINDERS

....
....
....
....
....
....

AUGUST ✤ SEPTEMBER

30 Monday

To lower blood pressure,
line the bottom of
your shoes with fresh
Spanish moss.

31 Tuesday

Wallpaper with
vertical stripes makes
a room seem taller.

1 Wednesday

Last Quarter

2 Thursday

*The truth is always
exciting. Speak it, then.
Life is dull without it.*
–Pearl S. Buck, American writer
(1892–1973)

SEPTEMBER • 2010

S	M	T	W	T	F	S
			1	2	3	4
5	6	7	8	9	10	11
12	13	14	15	16	17	18
19	20	21	22	23	24	25
26	27	28	29	30		

OCTOBER • 2010

S	M	T	W	T	F	S
					1	2
3	4	5	6	7	8	9
10	11	12	13	14	15	16
17	18	19	20	21	22	23
24	25	26	27	28	29	30
31						

Friday 3

Egg-ucation:
It is easier to separate yolks from whites when the eggs are cold.

Saturday 4

Q. *Why are fish so smart?*
A. Because they live in schools.

Sunday 5

There is at least one rotten apple in every barrel.

REMINDERS

SEPTEMBER with *The Old Farmer's Almanac*

125 Years Ago

SEPTEMBER 1885

If we could all raise our own seed, it would save us from much doubt and loss, for we should then know where we are.

—The Old Farmer's Almanac

Mercury and You

When Mercury is retrograde in Virgo:
Expect product delays, equipment breakdowns, and cranky coworkers. Double-check your work before calling it finished.

Current stage:
Mercury is retrograde in Virgo through September 12. It then is direct through December 9.

Rain in September is good for the farmer but poison to the grape growers.

MONTHLY REMINDERS

FULL MOON

SEPTEMBER 23

To Sioux tribes, this month's full Moon was the "Moon When Plums Are Scarlet."

Extended Car Care

If you plan to store your car indoors for an extended period, keep these tips in mind so that it can still be driven when you take it back out on the road:

■ Fill the gas tank and add a fuel stabilizer if the car is being stored during the winter.

■ Disconnect and remove the battery. Store it in an area where temperatures are stable and above freezing.

■ Put the car up on blocks and remove the tires and wheels to avoid getting flat spots.

■ Stuff crumpled aluminum foil into the tailpipe, the engine intake, and the fresh air intake to keep out mice and other critters looking for a winter home. Unlike cloth rags, aluminum foil does not make good nesting material for rodents.

■ Wax the car and then cover it with a breathable fabric.

SEPTEMBER

6 *Monday*

Labor Day

When your work speaks for itself, don't interrupt.

–Henry J. Kaiser, American industrialist (1882–1967)

7 *Tuesday*

Put a jar lid on the bottom of a double boiler; when the lid rattles, you'll know it's time to add more water.

8 *Wednesday*

New Moon

9 *Thursday*

Rosh Hashanah
Admission Day (Calif.)

The official state flower of California is the California poppy.

SEPTEMBER • 2010

S	M	T	W	T	F	S
			1	2	3	4
5	6	7	8	9	10	11
12	13	14	15	16	17	18
19	20	21	22	23	24	25
26	27	28	29	30		

OCTOBER • 2010

S	M	T	W	T	F	S
					1	2
3	4	5	6	7	8	9
10	11	12	13	14	15	16
17	18	19	20	21	22	23
24	25	26	27	28	29	30
31						

Friday **10**

On this day in 1935, *Popeye* aired for the first time, on NBC Radio.

Saturday **11**

Patriot Day

I look upon every day to be lost in which I do not make a new acquaintance.

–Dr. Samuel Johnson,
English writer (1709–84)

Sunday **12**

Grandparents Day

There are years that ask questions and years that answer.

–Zora Neale Hurston,
American writer (1891–1960)

REMINDERS

....

....

....

....

....

....

September

13 Monday

Time you enjoyed wasting is not wasted time.
—T. S. Eliot, British poet
(1888–1965)

14 Tuesday

*The 2011
Old Farmer's Almanac*
officially goes on
sale today.

15 Wednesday

First Quarter

16 Thursday

**Expect rain if chickens
roll in the sand.**

SEPTEMBER • 2010

S	M	T	W	T	F	S
			1	2	3	4
5	6	7	8	9	10	11
12	13	14	15	16	17	18
19	20	21	22	23	24	25
26	27	28	29	30		

OCTOBER • 2010

S	M	T	W	T	F	S
					1	2
3	4	5	6	7	8	9
10	11	12	13	14	15	16
17	18	19	20	21	22	23
24	25	26	27	28	29	30
31						

Constitution Day

Friday **17**

The United States Constitution is the oldest written national constitution still in effect today.

Yom Kippur

Saturday **18**

He is always right who suspects that he is always making mistakes.

–Spanish proverb

GREEN UP:

Sunday **19**

Save water by taking showers instead of baths.

REMINDERS

September

20 *Monday*

It is thought that
cleaning your ears with
a rooster feather will
make you go crazy.

21 *Tuesday*

International Day of Peace

*I believe that peace is
not merely an absence
of war, but the nurture
of human life. . . .*
–Jane Addams, American reformer
(1860–1935)

22 *Wednesday*

Autumnal Equinox

The Sun crosses the
equator on its
southward path at
11:09 P.M. EDT
today.

23 *Thursday*

Full Harvest Moon

SEPTEMBER • 2010							OCTOBER • 2010						
S	M	T	W	T	F	S	S	M	T	W	T	F	S
			1	2	3	4						1	2
5	6	7	8	9	10	11	3	4	5	6	7	8	9
12	13	14	15	16	17	18	10	11	12	13	14	15	16
19	20	21	22	23	24	25	17	18	19	20	21	22	23
26	27	28	29	30			24	25	26	27	28	29	30
							31						

Friday **24**

When putting your belongings in a storage unit, leave a center aisle to access items easily.

Saturday **25**

Indecision may or may not be my problem.

—Jimmy Buffett,
American musician (b. 1946)

Sunday **26**

One apple pie contains about two pounds of apples.

R E M I N D E R S

....
....
....
....
....
....

September

27 *Monday*

The study of proverbs is called paremiology.

28 *Tuesday*

Rose geranium leaves, when well dried, are equal to rose leaves for filling cushions and sachet bags.
–The Old Farmer's Almanac, 1916

29 *Wednesday*

On this day in 1907, actor Gene Autry was born.

30 *Thursday*

Last Quarter

The Easiest Thing You'll Do All Year!

How would you like to receive next year's elegant Engagement Calendar <u>PLUS</u> a copy of *The Old Farmer's Almanac* <u>AND</u> save the hassle of reordering?

Order your 2011 calendar today, and join our **Special No-Hassle Renewal Program:** Each year, we'll reserve your copy of The Old Farmer's Almanac Engagement Calendar, <u>PLUS</u> that year's edition of *The Old Farmer's Almanac* as our gift to you. We'll send you an advance notice of shipment as a reminder, and include a postage-paid reply card in case you have changes to your address or quantity, or wish to cancel your order. If you choose to receive your new calendar, you won't have to do a thing—we'll mail it (and your Almanac) in early September, along with your invoice.

You may cancel this program at any time with no further obligation, and will always have 30 days to respond to our reminder.

Order today, and we'll rush your 2011 Engagement Calendar to your doorstep and sign you up for our Special No-Hassle Renewal Program. Why wait? It's that easy!

FREE ALMANAC with your order, a $5.99 value!

Due to mailing requirements, we regret that we are unable to offer this program outside of the United States.

THREE EASY WAYS TO ORDER

 Online Shop.Almanac.com

 Mail Cut out, complete, and fold this form, tape, and mail.
Or, use your own envelope and mail to the address on the back of this form.

Phone Toll-free 1-800-ALMANAC, mention key A70EEC.

ORDERED BY:

_____
Name

_____
Address

_____
City / State / Zip

2011 calendars are scheduled to ship beginning in September 2010.

ORDER SUMMARY:

_____ copies SPECIAL RENEWAL OF11CEGC @ $14.99 $_____

Massachusetts (5%) or Illinois (6.25%) Sales Tax $_____

+ Shipping and Handling $ <u>4.95</u>

Key code: A70EEC   TOTAL ENCLOSED: $_____

☐ Bill me

☐ Check or money order enclosed

Charge my: ☐ Visa   ☐ MasterCard
☐ American Express   ☐ Discover/NOVUS

_____
Account Number   **Exp. Date**

_____
Signature (required for credit card orders)

A70EEC

For fastest service, go to Shop.Almanac.com

Name: _____

Address: _____

_____

City/Town: _____ State: _____ Zip: _____

☛ **RUSH!**
Order for
2011
Calendar
enclosed!

BUSINESS REPLY MAIL
FIRST-CLASS MAIL   PERMIT NO 572   FLAGLER BEACH FL

POSTAGE WILL BE PAID BY ADDRESSEE

**THE OLD FARMER'S ALMANAC
PO BOX 422453
PALM COAST FL 32142-8286**

Fold along this line. ⬆

After cutting this order form out of the book along the vertical dotted line, fold it in half along the horizontal dotted line. Please be sure to either complete the credit card information on the order form or enclose a check. Then tape the envelope closed along the three open edges. Do not send cash.

Cut along this line. ✂

Use clear tape on all three open sides to seal completely.

OCTOBER

OCTOBER • 2010

S	M	T	W	T	F	S
					1	2
3	4	5	6	7	8	9
10	11	12	13	14	15	16
17	18	19	20	21	22	23
24	25	26	27	28	29	30
31						

NOVEMBER • 2010

S	M	T	W	T	F	S
	1	2	3	4	5	6
7	8	9	10	11	12	13
14	15	16	17	18	19	20
21	22	23	24	25	26	27
28	29	30				

Q. *Why was the chicken thrown out of the baseball game?* **A.** The umpire suspected fowl play.

Friday 1

I live a very dull life here . . . indeed, I think I am more like a state prisoner than anything else.

–Martha Washington, U.S. First Lady (1731–1802)

Saturday 2

Test smoke alarms and fire extinguishers now, before the heating season starts.

Sunday 3

REMINDERS

....

....

....

....

....

....

125 Years Ago

OCTOBER 1885

It is a good time to do a little fall plowing. The teams are strong enough to turn over a deep furrow.

–The Old Farmer's Almanac

Mercury and You

When Mercury is retrograde in Libra:
Indecision reigns, so limit purchases—or risk returning them. Take time to refresh, relax, and rejuvenate.

Current stage:
Mercury is direct through December 9. It is not retrograde in Libra this year.

There are always 19 fine days in October.

MONTHLY REMINDERS

FULL MOON

OCTOBER 22

The Cheyenne called this month's full Moon the "Moon When the Water Begins to Freeze on the Edge of the Streams."

Winter Preparations

Take advantage of the warm fall days to prepare for winter:

- Make an appointment to have your chimney cleaned and inspected.

- Split and stack firewood. Gather and stockpile kindling. If an unsplittable log remains, use it as a Yule log.

- Remove window boxes, scrub them with a solution of water and bleach, and store for next year.

- Clean woodstove glass with a rag dampened with white vinegar.

- Apply stove black on a warm day so that you can open the doors and windows until the oily smell burns off.

- Remove window screens and wash the windows. Check the condition of storm windows and wash, if necessary.

OCTOBER

4 *Monday*

Child Health Day

Truths are not uttered
from behind masks.

—Greek proverb

5 *Tuesday*

The official state
flower of Arizona is
the saguaro cactus
blossom.

Arizona

6 *Wednesday*

Wednesday clearing,
clear till Sunday.

7 *Thursday*

New Moon

OCTOBER • 2010

S	M	T	W	T	F	S
					1	2
3	4	5	6	7	8	9
10	11	12	13	14	15	16
17	18	19	20	21	22	23
24	25	26	27	28	29	30
31						

NOVEMBER • 2010

S	M	T	W	T	F	S
	1	2	3	4	5	6
7	8	9	10	11	12	13
14	15	16	17	18	19	20
21	22	23	24	25	26	27
28	29	30				

All books are divisible into two classes: the books of the hour and the books of all time.

–John Ruskin, English critic (1819–1900)

Friday 8

Leif Eriksson Day

Saturday 9

Raking leaves burns about the same amount of calories as ballroom dancing.

Happy Birthday:

Sunday 10

In eastern Canada, children's noses are greased with butter on their birthdays to make them too slippery for bad luck to catch.

REMINDERS

....

....

....

....

....

....

OCTOBER

11 *Monday*

Columbus Day (observed)
Thanksgiving Day
(Canada)

Columbus brought
chickens to the New
World in 1493.

12 *Tuesday*

GREEN UP:
Create a natural wind
block around your
house with a row of
shrubs or evergreens,
such as hemlock,
cedar, or white pine.

13 *Wednesday*

Better a spoon of juice in
peace than a table laden
with food in quarrel.

—Yugoslavian proverb

14 *Thursday*

First Quarter

OCTOBER • 2010

S	M	T	W	T	F	S
					1	2
3	4	5	6	7	8	9
10	11	12	13	14	15	16
17	18	19	20	21	22	23
24	25	26	27	28	29	30
31						

NOVEMBER • 2010

S	M	T	W	T	F	S
	1	2	3	4	5	6
7	8	9	10	11	12	13
14	15	16	17	18	19	20
21	22	23	24	25	26	27
28	29	30				

In the 1600s, American colonists called apples "winter bananas."

Friday **15**

Fashion is architecture: It is a matter of proportions.
—Coco Chanel, French fashion designer (1883–1971)

Saturday **16**

A baby porcupine is a porcupette.

Sunday **17**

REMINDERS

....
....
....
....
....

OCTOBER

18 Monday

Alaska Day

To the lover of wilderness, Alaska is one of the most wonderful countries in the world.
—John Muir, American naturalist (1838–1914)

19 Tuesday

Before an intense workout, eat some honey. It will give you energy.

20 Wednesday

On this day in 1803, the United States ratified the Louisiana Purchase Treaty.

21 Thursday

It is time to stack your hay and corn
When the old donkey blows his horn.

OCTOBER • 2010

S	M	T	W	T	F	S
					1	2
3	4	5	6	7	8	9
10	11	12	13	14	15	16
17	18	19	20	21	22	23
24	25	26	27	28	29	30
31						

NOVEMBER • 2010

S	M	T	W	T	F	S
	1	2	3	4	5	6
7	8	9	10	11	12	13
14	15	16	17	18	19	20
21	22	23	24	25	26	27
28	29	30				

Full Hunter's Moon

Friday 22

Plant tulip bulbs twice as deep as their height.

Saturday 23

United Nations Day

Peace and tranquility are [worth] a thousand gold pieces.

—Chinese proverb

Sunday 24

REMINDERS

OCTOBER

25 *Monday*

26 *Tuesday*

To prevent rice or
pasta water from
boiling over, rub the
rim of the cooking pot
with butter.

27 *Wednesday*

When birds and
badgers are fat in October,
expect a cold winter.

28 *Thursday*

On this day in 2007,
the Boston Red Sox
won the World Series.

OCTOBER • 2010

S	M	T	W	T	F	S
					1	2
3	4	5	6	7	8	9
10	11	12	13	14	15	16
17	18	19	20	21	22	23
24	25	26	27	28	29	30
31						

NOVEMBER • 2010

S	M	T	W	T	F	S
	1	2	3	4	5	6
7	8	9	10	11	12	13
14	15	16	17	18	19	20
21	22	23	24	25	26	27
28	29	30				

Nevada Day

Friday 29

Nevada is the driest
state, with an average
of about 7 inches of
rain per year.

Last Quarter

Saturday 30

Halloween

Sunday 31

Pumpkins were
once thought to cure
snakebites.

REMINDERS

....

....

....

....

....

Complement this calendar with daily weather and Almanac wit and wisdom at Almanac.com.

125 Years Ago

NOVEMBER 1885

Pine boughs, old cornstalks, coarse straw, or eelgrass are handy to throw over the strawberry beds to help them stand the cold.

–The Old Farmer's Almanac

Mercury and You

When Mercury is retrograde in Scorpio:
Emotions rule—not common sense.
Avoid affairs of the heart. Your secrets may seep out.

❧

Current stage:
Mercury is direct through December 9.
It is not retrograde in Scorpio this year.

If the leaves of the trees and grapevines do not fall before Martin's Day [November 11], a cold winter may be expected.

MONTHLY REMINDERS

Chippewa tribes called this month's full Moon the "Freezing" Moon.

AROUND THE HOUSE

Evergreen Enhancements

❧

Not all evergreens are created equal. Their different forms and textures make them suitable for a variety of holiday decorations:

- Boxwood: Use in wreaths, roping, and floral arrangements.

- Holly: Clippings make great accents in floral arrangements.

- Pachysandra: Use for roping and decorations that need bunches of greens.

- Ivy: Let it trail over mantels or tuck sprigs into a wreath.

- Firs: The soft needles of Douglas and balsam firs wrap easily around staircases or drape across mantels.

- White pine: The long, soft needles make white pine ideal for swags draped over windows or mantels.

November

1 Monday

Throw dried peach pits into the fireplace; they will burn with a pleasant, fruity fragrance.

2 Tuesday

Election Day

Ancient Romans cast "no" votes with black beans and "yes" votes with white beans.

3 Wednesday

A misty morning may have a fine day.

4 Thursday

Will Rogers Day (Okla.)

We are all here for a spell; get all the good laughs you can.
—Will Rogers, American humorist (1879–1935)

NOVEMBER • 2010

S	M	T	W	T	F	S
	1	2	3	4	5	6
7	8	9	10	11	12	13
14	15	16	17	18	19	20
21	22	23	24	25	26	27
28	29	30				

DECEMBER • 2010

S	M	T	W	T	F	S
			1	2	3	4
5	6	7	8	9	10	11
12	13	14	15	16	17	18
19	20	21	22	23	24	25
26	27	28	29	30	31	

A dream of the new Moon promises wealth.

Friday 5

New Moon

Saturday 6

Daylight Saving Time ends at 2:00 A.M.

Remember to "fall back" by setting your clocks back 1 hour.

Sunday 7

REMINDERS

NOVEMBER

8 *Monday*

'Tis with our judgments
as our watches, none
go just alike, yet each
believes his own.
—Alexander Pope, English poet
(1688–1744)

9 *Tuesday*

When stars flicker in a
dark background, expect
rain or snow soon.

10 *Wednesday*

Egg-ucation:
On average, a hen lays
300 eggs per year.

11 *Thursday*

Veterans Day
Remembrance Day
(Canada)

Some men, if they have
twice as much to do,
will do it twice as well.
—The Old Farmer's Almanac,
1902

NOVEMBER • 2010

S	M	T	W	T	F	S
	1	2	3	4	5	6
7	8	9	10	11	12	13
14	15	16	17	18	19	20
21	22	23	24	25	26	27
28	29	30				

DECEMBER • 2010

S	M	T	W	T	F	S
			1	2	3	4
5	6	7	8	9	10	11
12	13	14	15	16	17	18
19	20	21	22	23	24	25
26	27	28	29	30	31	

Friday 12

Oil your sewing machine after about every 8 to 10 hours of sewing, unless your manual says otherwise.

First Quarter

Saturday 13

Sunday 14

Now is a good time to clean or replace furnace air filters.

REMINDERS

....

....

....

....

....

....

November

15 Monday

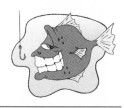

16 Tuesday

GREEN UP:
Resetting your thermostat from 72° to 65°F for 8 hours a day can cut your heating bill by up to 10 percent.

17 Wednesday

To test cranberries for freshness, drop one on the floor. If it bounces, most likely the batch is fresh.

18 Thursday

Flattery is all right so long as you don't inhale.
—Adlai E. Stevenson,
American politician (1900–65)

NOVEMBER • 2010

S	M	T	W	T	F	S
	1	2	3	4	5	6
7	8	9	10	11	12	13
14	15	16	17	18	19	20
21	22	23	24	25	26	27
28	29	30				

DECEMBER • 2010

S	M	T	W	T	F	S
			1	2	3	4
5	6	7	8	9	10	11
12	13	14	15	16	17	18
19	20	21	22	23	24	25
26	27	28	29	30	31	

Friday **19**

Discovery Day (Puerto
Rico)

**Expect good luck
if you receive an orange
as a gift.**

Saturday **20**

*Art serves to rinse
out our eyes.*
–Karl Kraus, Austrian satirist
(1874–1936)

Sunday **21**

Full Beaver Moon

REMINDERS

NOVEMBER

22 *Monday*

Well, if I called the wrong number, why did you answer the phone?
–James Thurber, American writer (1894–1961)

23 *Tuesday*

On this day in 1936, the first issue of *LIFE* magazine was published.

24 *Wednesday*

The free thinking of one age is the common sense of the next.
–Matthew Arnold, English poet (1822–88)

25 *Thursday*

Thanksgiving Day

For fluffy mashed potatoes: After boiling, drain, place paper towels inside the pot lid, cover, and let sit for a few minutes before mashing.

NOVEMBER • 2010

S	M	T	W	T	F	S
	1	2	3	4	5	6
7	8	9	10	11	12	13
14	15	16	17	18	19	20
21	22	23	24	25	26	27
28	29	30				

DECEMBER • 2010

S	M	T	W	T	F	S
			1	2	3	4
5	6	7	8	9	10	11
12	13	14	15	16	17	18
19	20	21	22	23	24	25
26	27	28	29	30	31	

Acadian Day (La.)

Friday **26**

*Education is hanging
around until you've
caught on.*

–Robert Frost, American poet
(1874–1963)

Saturday **27**

To protect against
witches, folks in the
Middle Ages stuffed
fennel into their
doors' keyholes.

Last Quarter

Sunday **28**

REMINDERS

....
....
....
....
....

29 Monday

Three feet of ice are not frozen in one day.
—*Chinese proverb*

30 Tuesday

If you are able to touch the tips of your little finger and forefinger over the back of your hand, you can have any sweetheart you like.

1 Wednesday

Q. *Why did the chicken cross the road?*
A. Because the rooster egged her on.

2 Thursday

First day of Chanukah

To keep shelled nuts from becoming rancid, store them in an airtight container in the refrigerator or freezer.

DECEMBER • 2010

S	M	T	W	T	F	S
			1	2	3	4
5	6	7	8	9	10	11
12	13	14	15	16	17	18
19	20	21	22	23	24	25
26	27	28	29	30	31	

JANUARY • 2011

S	M	T	W	T	F	S
						1
2	3	4	5	6	7	8
9	10	11	12	13	14	15
16	17	18	19	20	21	22
23	24	25	26	27	28	29
30	31					

*I want to live my life,
not record it.*

–Jacqueline Kennedy Onassis,
U.S. First Lady (1929–94)

Friday 3

Every pomegranate
contains exactly
840 seeds.

Saturday 4

New Moon

Sunday 5

REMINDERS

125 Years Ago

DECEMBER 1885

But the days are short now, and we must make the most of them so as to have some time left for reading and study.

—The Old Farmer's Almanac

Mercury and You

When Mercury is retrograde in Capricorn: Avoid buying, selling, or renting real estate. Expect problems with paperwork, packing, and movers. Reunite with family or take a vacation.

When Mercury is retrograde in Sagittarius: Avoid making travel plans, as delays, long lines, and lost directions are common. Take care of local affairs with patience and humor.

Current stage:
In December, Mercury is direct through the 9th. It then is retrograde in Capricorn from the 10th through the 18th and in Sagittarius from the 19th through the 30th. It is direct from December 31 through March 29, 2011.

The more snow, the more healthy the season.

MONTHLY REMINDERS

Yuchi tribes called this month's full Moon the "Middle of Winter" Moon.

AROUND THE HOUSE

A Full House

Keep these items on hand to meet the demands as guests pile into your house during the holidays:

- **Folding chairs.** When not in use, store them under a bed, in the back of a closet, or on their sides behind the couch.

- **Small folding table or card table.** In addition to being a kids' table, it can hold additional food if your dining table is too crowded or if you are serving a buffet.

- **Large, clean, white sheet.** In a pinch, use it as a tablecloth.

- **Fire extinguisher.** Even the best laid plans can go astray.

December

6 *Monday*

When doubling a recipe, add the original amount of salt and then taste before adding more.

7 *Tuesday*

National Pearl Harbor Remembrance Day

Don't forget to fill the bird feeder when winter storms are forecast.

8 *Wednesday*

Islamic New Year

The surest way to destroy your own health is to be constantly drinking to that of other people.
–The Old Farmer's Almanac, *1860*

9 *Thursday*

Happy Birthday:

In Israel, the birthday child sits in a chair that is raised and lowered once for each year of age, plus once for good luck.

DECEMBER • 2010

S	M	T	W	T	F	S
			1	2	3	4
5	6	7	8	9	10	11
12	13	14	15	16	17	18
19	20	21	22	23	24	25
26	27	28	29	30	31	

JANUARY • 2011

S	M	T	W	T	F	S
						1
2	3	4	5	6	7	8
9	10	11	12	13	14	15
16	17	18	19	20	21	22
23	24	25	26	27	28	29
30	31					

Friday is the best or worst day of the week.

Friday **10**

I find television very educating. Every time somebody turns on the set, I go into the other room and read a book.

–Groucho Marx, American comedian (1890–1977)

Saturday **11**

One's blessings are not known until lost.

Sunday **12**

REMINDERS

....
....
....
....
....
....

DECEMBER

13 *Monday*

First Quarter

14 *Tuesday*

GREEN UP:
To save electricity,
use a timer on your
indoor and outdoor
holiday lights.

15 *Wednesday*

Bill of Rights Day

Not every good scholar
is a good
schoolmaster.

16 *Thursday*

Egg-ucation:
If hard-cooked eggs
have a greenish rim
around the yolk, they
may be overcooked.

DECEMBER • 2010

S	M	T	W	T	F	S
			1	2	3	4
5	6	7	8	9	10	11
12	13	14	15	16	17	18
19	20	21	22	23	24	25
26	27	28	29	30	31	

JANUARY • 2011

S	M	T	W	T	F	S
						1
2	3	4	5	6	7	8
9	10	11	12	13	14	15
16	17	18	19	20	21	22
23	24	25	26	27	28	29
30	31					

Wright Brothers Day

Friday 17

The official state flower of North Carolina is the dogwood.

Never be afraid to sit awhile and think.

—Lorraine Hansberry,
American playwright (1930–65)

Saturday 18

The word "tomato" is from the ancient Aztec word *tomatl.*

Sunday 19

REMINDERS

December

20 *Monday*

*To travel hopefully
is a better thing
than to arrive.*

—Robert Louis Stevenson,
Scottish writer (1850–94)

21 *Tuesday*

**Winter Solstice
Full Cold Moon**

22 *Wednesday*

*He is a fool who can
not be angry;
but he is a wise man
who will not.*

—Lucius Annaeus Seneca, Roman
statesman (c. 4 B.C.–A.D. 65)

23 *Thursday*

After its first 24 hours
indoors, the average
Christmas tree may
drink up to a quart of
water daily.

DECEMBER • 2010

S M T W T F S
1 2 3 4
5 6 7 8 9 10 11
12 13 14 15 16 17 18
19 20 21 22 23 24 25
26 27 28 29 30 31

JANUARY • 2011

S M T W T F S
1
2 3 4 5 6 7 8
9 10 11 12 13 14 15
16 17 18 19 20 21 22
23 24 25 26 27 28 29
30 31

Friday **24**

If you suffer backaches, empty your pockets, wear loose clothing, and don't cross your legs.

Saturday **25**

Christmas Day

Christmas isn't a season. It's a feeling.
–Edna Ferber, American writer
(1887–1968)

Sunday **26**

Boxing Day (Canada)
First day of Kwanzaa

On this day in 1974, Congress amended legislation to allow girls to play in Little League baseball.

REMINDERS

....
....
....
....
....
....

December ❧ January 2011

27 *Monday*

28 *Tuesday*

The average cow
produces enough milk
each day to fill about
120 glasses.

29 *Wednesday*

To get rid of hiccups,
wet a small piece of
a brown paper bag and
put it on your forehead.

30 *Thursday*

Humans shed about
600,000 skin cells
per hour.

DECEMBER • 2010

S	M	T	W	T	F	S
			1	2	3	4
5	6	7	8	9	10	11
12	13	14	15	16	17	18
19	20	21	22	23	24	25
26	27	28	29	30	31	

JANUARY • 2011

S	M	T	W	T	F	S
						1
2	3	4	5	6	7	8
9	10	11	12	13	14	15
16	17	18	19	20	21	22
23	24	25	26	27	28	29
30	31					

Friday

31

Today, the sixth
day of Kwanzaa,
communities celebrate
with a feast called
a karamu.

Saturday

1

New Year's Day

Babies born today
will have good luck
throughout their
whole life.

Sunday

2

*Life is the garment we
continually alter, but
which never seems to fit.*

–David McCord, American poet
(1897–1997)

R EMINDERS

....

....

....

....

....

....

2011 Advance Planner

bold = U.S. Federal and/or Canadian National holidays

JANUARY • 2011

S	M	T	W	T	F	S
						1
2	3	4	5	6	7	8
9	10	11	12	13	14	15
16	**17**	18	19	20	21	22
23	24	25	26	27	28	29
30	31					

FEBRUARY • 2011

S	M	T	W	T	F	S
	1	2	3	4	5	
6	7	8	9	10	11	12
13	14	15	16	17	18	19
20	**21**	22	23	24	25	26
27	28					

MARCH • 2011

S	M	T	W	T	F	S
	1	2	3	4	5	
6	7	8	9	10	11	12
13	14	15	16	17	18	19
20	21	22	23	24	25	26
27	28	29	30	31		

APRIL • 2011

S	M	T	W	T	F	S
					1	2
3	4	5	6	7	8	9
10	11	12	13	14	15	16
17	18	19	20	21	**22**	23
24	**25**	26	27	28	29	30

MAY • 2011

S	M	T	W	T	F	S
1	2	3	4	5	6	7
8	9	10	11	12	13	14
15	16	17	18	19	20	21
22	**23**	24	25	26	27	28
29	**30**	31				

JUNE • 2011

S	M	T	W	T	F	S
			1	2	3	4
5	6	7	8	9	10	11
12	13	14	15	16	17	18
19	20	21	22	23	24	25
26	27	28	29	30		

JULY • 2011

S	M	T	W	T	F	S
					1	2
3	**4**	5	6	7	8	9
10	11	12	13	14	15	16
17	18	19	20	21	22	23
24	25	26	27	28	29	30
31						

AUGUST • 2011

S	M	T	W	T	F	S
	1	2	3	4	5	6
7	8	9	10	11	12	13
14	15	16	17	18	19	20
21	22	23	24	25	26	27
28	29	30	31			

SEPTEMBER • 2011

S	M	T	W	T	F	S
				1	2	3
4	**5**	6	7	8	9	10
11	12	13	14	15	16	17
18	19	20	21	22	23	24
25	26	27	28	29	30	

OCTOBER • 2011

S	M	T	W	T	F	S
						1
2	3	4	5	6	7	8
9	**10**	11	12	13	14	15
16	17	18	19	20	21	22
23	24	25	26	27	28	29
30	31					

NOVEMBER • 2011

S	M	T	W	T	F	S
		1	2	3	4	5
6	7	8	9	10	**11**	12
13	14	15	16	17	18	19
20	21	22	23	**24**	25	26
27	28	29	30			

DECEMBER • 2011

S	M	T	W	T	F	S
				1	2	3
4	5	6	7	8	9	10
11	12	13	14	15	16	17
18	19	20	21	22	23	24
25	**26**	27	28	29	30	31

2012 Advance Planner

bold = *U.S. Federal and/or Canadian National holidays*

JANUARY • 2012

S	M	T	W	T	F	S
1	2	3	4	5	6	7
8	9	10	11	12	13	14
15	**16**	17	18	19	20	21
22	23	24	25	26	27	28
29	30	31				

FEBRUARY • 2012

S	M	T	W	T	F	S
			1	2	3	4
5	6	7	8	9	10	11
12	13	14	15	16	17	18
19	**20**	21	22	23	24	25
26	27	28	29			

MARCH • 2012

S	M	T	W	T	F	S
				1	2	3
4	5	6	7	8	9	10
11	12	13	14	15	16	17
18	19	20	21	22	23	24
25	26	27	28	29	30	31

APRIL • 2012

S	M	T	W	T	F	S
1	2	3	4	5	**6**	7
8	**9**	10	11	12	13	14
15	16	17	18	19	20	21
22	23	24	25	26	27	28
29	30					

MAY • 2012

S	M	T	W	T	F	S
		1	2	3	4	5
6	7	8	9	10	11	12
13	14	15	16	17	18	19
20	**21**	22	23	24	25	26
27	**28**	29	30	31		

JUNE • 2012

S	M	T	W	T	F	S
					1	2
3	4	5	6	7	8	9
10	11	12	13	14	15	16
17	18	19	20	21	22	23
24	25	26	27	28	29	30

JULY • 2012

S	M	T	W	T	F	S
1	2	3	**4**	5	6	7
8	9	10	11	12	13	14
15	16	17	18	19	20	21
22	23	24	25	26	27	28
29	30	31				

AUGUST • 2011

S	M	T	W	T	F	S
			1	2	3	4
5	6	7	8	9	10	11
12	13	14	15	16	17	18
19	20	21	22	23	24	25
26	27	28	29	30	31	

SEPTEMBER • 2012

S	M	T	W	T	F	S
						1
2	**3**	4	5	6	7	8
9	10	11	12	13	14	15
16	17	18	19	20	21	22
23	24	25	26	27	28	29
30						

OCTOBER • 2012

S	M	T	W	T	F	S
	1	2	3	4	5	6
7	**8**	9	10	11	12	13
14	15	16	17	18	19	20
21	22	23	24	25	26	27
28	29	30	31			

NOVEMBER • 2012

S	M	T	W	T	F	S
				1	2	3
4	5	6	7	8	9	10
11	12	13	14	15	16	17
18	19	20	21	**22**	23	24
25	26	27	28	29	30	

DECEMBER • 2012

S	M	T	W	T	F	S
						1
2	3	4	5	6	7	8
9	10	11	12	13	14	15
16	17	18	19	20	21	22
23	24	**25**	**26**	27	28	29
30	31					

Complement this calendar with daily weather and Almanac wit and wisdom at Almanac.com.

Birthdays and Anniversaries

Name	Birthday	Anniversary

Addresses and Phone Numbers

Name _____   Home _____
Address _____   Work _____
_____   Cell _____
E-mail _____   Fax _____
Web site _____

Name _____   Home _____
Address _____   Work _____
_____   Cell _____
E-mail _____   Fax _____
Web site _____

Name _____   Home _____
Address _____   Work _____
_____   Cell _____
E-mail _____   Fax _____
Web site _____

Name _____   Home _____
Address _____   Work _____
_____   Cell _____
E-mail _____   Fax _____
Web site _____

Name _____   Home _____
Address _____   Work _____
_____   Cell _____
E-mail _____   Fax _____
Web site _____

Name _____   Home _____
Address _____   Work _____
_____   Cell _____
E-mail _____   Fax _____
Web site _____

Emergency Numbers

In case of emergency, notify:

Name _____ Relationship _____

Address _____

_____

Phone _____ E-mail _____

Police Department _____

Fire Department _____

Ambulance _____

Hospital _____

Poison Control _____

Physician _____

Dentist _____

Veterinarian _____

Pharmacy _____

Clergy _____

Electric Company _____

Electrician _____

Plumber _____

Auto Mechanic _____

Baby-sitter _____

School(s) _____

Insurance:

   Auto _____

   Health _____

   Dental _____

   Homeowner's _____

Other _____

_____

_____

_____

_____

_____